Contents Page

Introduction

We have most likely all been there without a job, where the possibilities seem small, luckily possibilities are always there, we just have to notice them, we can learn to become our own possibilities by creating them.

Society is sometimes misunderstood within this current time 2017; there have been so many changes many have impacted us for the better and some unfortunately for the worst. Within our worst moments we can find real courage that brings upon us a strength that pushes us to overcome our worst fears to find new opportunities and develop ourselves so we can achieve our goals.

Lets address the issue at hand you picked up this piece of information because you want to take a step into self employment or business, this can be somewhat scary, well I felt a bit scared changing over to becoming self employed, I wasn't sure whether it was better being on job seekers allowance or doing what I am currently doing now. If I waited to find employment maybe I would still be on Job seekers allowance, then I would have never created employment for myself or for other people, plus I would have to attend those mandatory work schemes.

Truth is if you've found this piece of information then you have what it takes to enter the world of self employment, do your

research, know the majority of the steps you l
before you take it, this way you make sure tha
your emotional and physical health there's no
worrying which creates stress and illness with
self employed folks eliminate worry by preparing, preparing
then preparing some more.

I truly hope that you will find this information useful, that it will
help you to view yourself as the success that you are knowing
that Rome wasn't build in a day, they had to work long and
hard.

Chapter 1: Creating the Idea

In order to start anything you have to want to do it, I don't mean that I'll do it for a few weeks then quit attitude, I mean the this is it and I'm going to stick to it attitude, that's the one that you will need to persevere and to keep winning even when it seems like you're not. So you want to do this, you really want to become self employed, to do this you must be a creative person and if you're not creative then you need to become creative, brave, determined, fearless and ready to learn, you will also need a lot of faith.

Truth is anything you can think of as an idea has probably been thought of already, having an idea is important however knowing yourself is even more important, there's no point starting something that you're not going to like and to be fair you may like it for a couple of weeks even months but what will keep you in business for years, that's if you want to be, well for me I asked myself the question If I was to do anything and not get paid for it then what would that be, for me this was cleaning I find that when I clean it feels like it purifies my mind body and soul. What would you do for free? Who would be willing to pay for it? How much do you think you should charge for it? I charge ten pounds an hour pay staff eight pounds an hour so the business keeps two pounds an hour, when I work jobs I get paid ten

pounds an hour which has since changed my cleaners now get paid £10.00 an hour and the business can make anything between £1.50-£3.50 an hour because I love my cleaners and I know they are worth more than minimum wage.

Some of you may have ideas that you will be charging thirty five pounds an hour or less or maybe you will be selling a product instead of a service, your services may be priced at £1000 or more. The questions I asked previously about what would you do for free etc are called coaching questions and may have other names however these questions are used to find out your internal dreams and goals so you do not end up just doing something because society or other people think it is a good idea, these questions are there to help you find your highest life purposes and goals. Ultimately I know that I was created by God therefore I am learning to consult God more regarding my purpose as doing it Gods way helps me to be truly fulfilled, money doesn't make pain or anger go away at times, life is also very difficult so I stay close to God in order for me to fully accomplish my purpose, if you don't believe in God then that is ok that is between you and your creator.

Find the time to think about what type of business you would like to create through being self employed, if you are unable to think of an idea then you can Google "need a business idea" look for the one that says here are 55- by Entrepreneur.com   cleaning is actually on their list and so is dog walking, I didn't participate in this process as I knew that I loved cleaning plus I was doing some self employed work for a cleaning company, I find these agencies a useful thing, you want to think of an idea or find yourself however we have to eat and provide shelter for ourselves so sometimes at the start of your business you sometimes need to work for someone else, so if a client cancels you will still receive an income elsewhere, there are self employed jobs out there also temporary jobs can come in useful however the option of temporary jobs can interfere with your benefits or tax credits so self employed jobs is a good avenue while building your self employed business.

If your still wanting to become self employed then once you know what you want to do and many of you probably already know what it is that you will be doing, then this option can be done without spending a lot of money and this will include your marketing budget also if you have fifty pounds then that would be a large budget compared to what I started with.

The cleaning business Home Zone Cleaning is the third business I have set up, over a period of 4 years. A cleaning business may not be for you but remember to ask yourself what you love doing, are you good at it and if you're not then probably don't do it as your customers may not be pleased with the job however if you're a perfectionist then still do it as your standards are probably going to be way higher than that of your customers. Be practical if you want to be a plumber or electrician or other trades where you know you need a qualification then please wait until you are adequately trained.

This is the reason why I choose cleaning, you don't need to be qualified to practice, I don't normally need my own tools and I can find jobs for others in the same systematic ways I find myself jobs which is very useful because by helping others to make money I also make some for myself. Whenever I am thinking about business ideas I think how can I benefit others and also benefit myself, I think having good intentions in how you do your business is useful in order to continue to run an ethical business.

I hope you find what you love doing, so let's find out how to make the rest happen and let's remember to keep it Simple!

List things you love doing

1.

2.

3.

4.

5.

<u>List your Whys</u>

(Why do you want to become self employed?)

1.

2.

3.

4.

5.

Chapter 2: Managing your finances

Often the dreaded word (finances), the world says were are broke, the bankers the MPs, it's all that we hear about, if you decide to go self employed and you know you need to attract new clients then the first thing that you may think is no one has any money so how will they pay for your services. This very statement alone may stop us from trying to set up our business because in our minds we have already lost the battle, "your just not good enough" we all hear similar voices only some thoughts create Gold.

Some people are born lucky however some people have to work quite hard at it or you can learn to work the SMART way (which is learning how to do less but gain more), so you're biggest Finances is your mind, feed it with the right information and see your finances expand.

OK so now to work out your bills!!

If you are receiving Jobs seekers allowance then you may be getting housing benefit support which you can also get once you become self employed. Luckily once you become self employed you can access Working Tax Credit, you will need to be over 25 years old and over, if you're working on your business say 39 hours a week: not to worry you don't need to be working with your clients all this time (Phew) this is time spent on marketing, planning, researching also forecasting and you can probably think of many other things to spend that 39 hours on. Lets say your projected earnings will be roughly £4,000 a year you should get around £50 a week from working tax credit which is about £70 less a month than Job seekers allowance however hopefully you will start earning that extra income in no time, £4000 may seem small as your first years earnings however we need to take into account that you will be receiving housing benefit and working tax credit, I believe there are also good options for individuals with disabilities that want to start a business to find out more please contact the job centre or do some research online or through gov.uk.

If you are earning under £5,965 then there is no need to pay class 2 national insurance rates as your earnings is below the threshold although you can still choose to, so if you receive an invoice for this then contact them via the details on invoice/letter and kindly explain your situation. I am very sorry to say that in this game many people will not tell you what our rights are we have to go searching for them, other people have travelled the path, so a lot of useful information is available it is just hidden so find your inner detective. You are still entitled to housing benefit if you are self employed! You will need to have a tenancy agreement in your name, all you need to do is get in touch with your local council and they will tell you how it's done, most likely you will need to provide evidence of bank statements, also a forecast of your earnings which is your profit and loss account, the council should provide you with this form so all you need do is put pen to paper and you will likely need a passport or driving license for identification.

Normally you will need to update your council forecasted income records every six months again they will ask for proof of your income normally they will ask for your bank statements, I believe it's every year working tax credit will send you a renewal pack which you would ensure the information is correct, if not you are expected to amend the information and return form, failure to return a form will normally result in your tax credit awards being stopped.

If you are paying over 1 pound on your credit card /store cards then you don't need to, especially if you are on JSA and are unable to afford it, contact National Debt Helpline who will send you sample letters that you will then forward to your credit/store card supplier, to be fair you can just phone them up and tell them you can only afford 1 a month to help to make your finances more manageable or you can send them an email so this becomes free, normally you have to search online for the companies email address.

What I found useful throughout my self employed journey is recording my income and expenses to be fair I don't record this information all the time however if I do feel that my finances will be stretched then I sit down and calculate my total income and expenses, normally I never have to borrow any money, I just know that I have to spent a certain amount on certain items, not knowing where I am with my finances means I do not know who I am, it could also mean that it strains your relationship with people because you become stressed, by recording this information we eliminate the stress and if you know you will need an extra £5 then maybe spend less elsewhere as I like to be independent and not borrow from friends or families.

As you begin to grow your business you should have more disposable income lets just always say, remember those days where you needed a pound for a loaf of bread and couldn't afford it, the reason why many of us could not afford something so cheap is because we were not good at managing our money, if we saw something we were quick to purchase it, I love to spend on myself so what I do is I became or was naturally a barging hunter, many of my clothes including jeans cost one pound, it's how you wear your clothes, and sometimes I set a rule in place that I will not buy anything other than necessities for about 2-3 month and on the 4th month I would give myself an allowance so I can be really happy and buy really pretty things.

I have reached the point now that I no longer invest too much in buying clothes as I have so many, therefore when I can I keep my money I do, as sometimes you may be in a position to help someone else through hardship and you never know when that same person can provide you with assistance and personally it's better to invest in the life and growth of my business rather than material things as in the future the business will benefit more people although I do believe it's important to look after our appearances as we are the face of the business.

As Mr Islam said, think wisely always think wisely about how you spend your money and when you do a job for other people do it as well as you would when do it for yourself.

Always know where you are with your finances so you are able to pay your bills on time, when I first started I had finished all my savings (this was due to the fact that I retired myself for 6 months and was unable to follow through with my next business venture however I thank God as that path may not have been the right one), I found it so hard financially, it was about on the 4th week that I became financially ok again, literally I struggled why because I took my eye of the ball. Always stay focused with your life plans, sometimes we will feel down in the dumps just never stay there for too long otherwise you will be lost there and it will take you ten times longer to get out of that situation.

Working out your finances

1. Expenses (things you pay out for I.e. food, gas, buss pass)

List all your expenses and then add them together

2. Income (money you receive I.e. job seekers allowance, self employment, tax credits)

List all your income then add them together

3. Minus your expenses from your income then you can see how much money you do or don't have. Follow this process for as many months as you need to in order to be able to budget effectively.

Chapter 3: Becoming self employed and employing staff

To become self employed you need to register, this link is useful
https://www.gov.uk/set-up-sole-trader
 The link helps you to get registered. Once you successfully register
you will be given a unique tax reference number which will probably
arrive in the post, this number allows you to apply for working tax
credit, feel free to get working tax credit to post you a form even
while you are in the planning stage of the business as sometimes it
can take two weeks to be delivered as this credit will be one of your
main source of income ,you need to have the processes and your
finances well planned out as your working tax credit could take a
couple of weeks to be processed.

A very important thing to remember once you become self employed
is to fill in your self assessment tax return form either online or on
paper, the deadline is later when doing it online, usually as soon as
they allow me to complete the form I do so as this is something that
can be easily forgotten which means that high charges will have to be
paid if the form is sent in late, and remember when you first start you
have to be sent several passwords in order to enter your user area so
it is very important that you give yourself time that if you need to ask
for passwords to be sent that you are able to do so. Basically with
everything in the business just train yourself to action everything
straight away therefore you will always be on top of your business
and your business will never be on top of you. Remember that you
can set reminders on your phone with alarms attached because no

one expects you to remember everything you have to do you just need to put systems in place to make the business run smoother.

When you register its normally as a sole trader, this is the simplest method that I have found and over time we may decide that a different business model will be more effective, normally you are able to trade for 3 months without registering your business, I do not think this applies if you are on JSA as if you are receiving money from your business then you are in breach of your benefit, JSA still offers an employment support service where you will receive mentoring and you get a certain amount of money when you first sign off benefits up until maybe 6 weeks so this is a good opportunity , as they may provide courses, once you enroll on a course then the organisation may be giving out grant funding which you do not need to pay back, I received £500 from an organisation many moons ago when starting my hairdressing company, also depending on your age you may be able to apply to the princess trust for grant funding, these opportunities are always changing but believe me they are out there, at first they are hard to find and obtain but when you know where to look you may be surprised at what you find, I wasn't going to but I thought that I would let you know that there are different options other than getting a loan(for me getting a loan was not a wise choice while starting my business), you are what you think about, why because what you think helps to create your actions and how you think affects how your plans are executed so your thoughts are a key driver in what and how we achieve our goals. Build your self esteem and confidence and you will build your business. Think creatively, when I am not in a creative mood I employ Google, such a large engine and its free, absolutely brilliant!

So employing staff, technically I do not employ staff if you go down this route you have to contribute to their national insurance and you are liable for everything and anything that happens, I offer opportunities to other self employed cleaners. In order to generate a list of cleaners I posted ads in corner shops mainly now I post adverts on Facebook, to make sure I protect the customer I ask the cleaner to provide me with two references of people they clean for and a copy of their passport or driving license which is then sent to my email address, you can purchase data holding insurance online for around £35. I only send customer details to cleaners once I have received all the information that I have requested, I have learned to manage cleaners better now so I ask cleaners what their postcodes are, the days and times that they are available so I can match jobs more affectively, I store the details on my phone and move them to different devices via my email, as when you are on the go it is vital that you have these information, if one of your clients needs a temporary cleaner then by having the customers details on your excel spreadsheet you can just collect the address and send to the temporary cleaner, I generally just text the cleaner the time and day how many hours and the postcode of the job so I keep the customers confidential information secure, once the cleaner accepts the job I then send through the customers full address and telephone number.

Quite often the cleaner gets paid cash or through their bank, I then ask the cleaner to pay me a certain amount i.e. £1.50 per hour into my bank account and there you have it a cost effective way of growing your business, as there is only so many hours you alone can work in a day and if you are getting surplus customers why tell them you are unable to help just get someone else to do it for you so you get more happy customers and hopefully more money.

Chapter 4: Advertising, continuous learning and developing systems

This is not as hard as we may think it is, truth is if we see something as hard then it becomes hard making it also impossible to create those amazing advertising Ideas, I am currently sat on the bus and working on this chapter when I notice a man outside a hairdresser handing out flyers, usually I would think that no one would take one however he had on a nice smile and I saw someone take a flyer meaning that in future I will deliver this same type of marketing, there are going to be instances where you walk into a shop and see a good promotion which you then may think that you will implement in your own business because many great ideas are already in action and noticing other companies marketing strategies is an awesome thing, it's likely the reason they are doing that strategy is probably because they have done it before and it works, when I find more time or make time or reprioritize what I think is important then I will look at marketing strategies done by big branded companies and take from their models which will help to strengthen and transform my own brand.

For me one of the most basic forms of advertising with the least cost attached to it is word of mouth, if you have friends and family that may benefit from your service then tell them about it, this actually comes in handy even though my cleaning services may not be needed by my peeps (people) that doesn't mean they are not helping me , for instance some of the people that I know have asked me to help find them cleaning work and its always handy to have extra staff also by communicating your goals to people that care you may benefit from them making valuable suggestions or further down the line they may make recommendations for staff or customers, you'll be surprised! This way there is no slacking off as your family and friends will ask for updates about what you are up to, giving you that much needed motivational encouragement which helps you to feel loved thus helping you to do more and achieve your dreams.

I notice that when I give 10% to my marketing strategies I get 10% back which is not a large percentage of new customers or cleaners so my return is minimum however when I start to increase my business efforts to 30-40% I see a difference in how many clients I receive, I don't think that I have invested over 50% in the business at one given period as I am constantly on the go working at times and do not believe in burning my candles from both ends.

At times I have not pushed because of fear of my strategy not working which creates tension in the body. As I grow through learning new strategies and self reflection I am able to see myself achieving my goals, I often stumble across new ideas that once implemented will enable me to recruit new cleaners or clients.

Sometimes it takes a few weeks or two to see the fruits of your labor however sometimes we have to ask ourselves the question how often have we planted a seed and in grew in 20 minutes, the truth is it often depends on the seed, if we know which strategies we are implementing then we often know how this seed will grow especially if it has already been implemented and the outcome has been analysed. When implementing our strategies or just being involved in the day to day running of our business and lives we need to adopt optimism, hope and faith to be able to persevere, to have determination, become more resourceful and become very courageous otherwise as soon as we face a challenge we are likely to want to give up, not knowing we were just 2 feet away from seeing results.

Most of us use social media if you do not currently then it may be useful to get acquainted with such platforms as Twitter, Facebook, YouTube, Pinterest, the list is currently endless, you don't necessarily need to use all of them at once, if you are technically clued up then do your thing as I assume the more platforms you use the more your client group will grow, if you communicate to Facebook groups in a way that they can interact to then I know that you can obtain clients from this social media platform, luckily there are loads of videos especially on you tube that helps you to learn how to develop these skills. The main social media I use to advertise is Facebook, this platform offers a selections of groups like Beckenham and Penge mums, I choose this group as a lot of work from home mums may be able to afford cleaning services as their time has more value when spent on their business rather than cleaning, I have also added other groups that I can advertise on, I will be adding more groups as this is a great free platform to reach millions of people and also acts as a great way to drive traffic to your website.

At first the outcome showed that this strategy of advertising through Facebook was not successful, I have since learnt to visit the Vistaprint website and develop flyers that I then crop on my phone, cropping is basically just reducing the seize so you are not able to see the search bar and other things that the screenshot captures, I also edit or adjust the brightness or sharpness etc in order to make the words look and feel great, well I do try. Using vista print flyers on Facebook gives the adverts a professional finish and since then I have gained both cleaners and clients, at times potential customers may not interact with your post however they may phone you at a later date so remember to ask the client where they saw your advert. I have yet to use the other platforms to advertise, I currently know that I am very busy and like to have a great work life balance and with the current rise in mental health I tend to take small strides instead of larger strides, many people have grown their business rapidly by taking risks and being much more motivated which for me is awesome as that works for that person. I will definitely eventually utilize these other platforms as this will help to stimulate growth within my business; the joy of this is that there is space to grow which is an important thing.

This is my latest Facebook advert I think it is so cute however next time I may use an advert which anchors my business, say an advert with a mop and bucket.

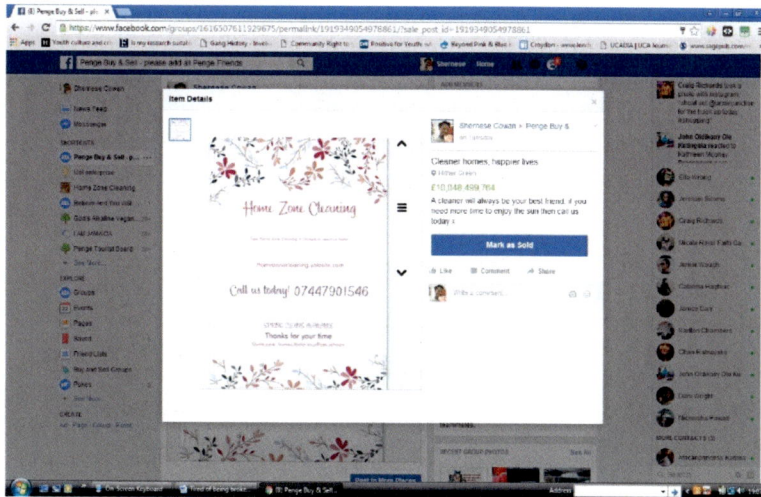

Let's face it, even though I am often shy about it "whisper_ I'm self employed" well now I shout it from the roof top because the strategies works, we have ventured into self employment because we are driven to create a business so why not go further and grow our business, this often happens by learning something new which allows us to implement new strategies and this doesn't necessarily mean that you need to go back to university or college as you may just be obtaining a debt for something you could probably learn from Google unless you need to learn something like plumbing then please do find your nearest educational institution. University or college is a great place to be a part of and if you know you need to do this then do it because you are creating and controlling your own reality just see it from an analytical brain and once you know what steps you need to take then take them.

Another business strategy that I use is my main Facebook picture, I normally place one of my adverts as my profile picture, even though I am currently using vista print to design my adverts I will try out other companies in order to change things up and add a bit of spice, the vista print flyer maker is so useful, I have just decided that I would create an advert and place it on my website making it look even more professional and beautiful, see the to do list just gets longer.

I have decided to grow my business slowly (organically) as this is the latest fashion, no really it due to the fact I have to deal with phones calls, updating systems, reply to emails and this is something I was not used to doing, I'm the type of girl that likes to take a vacation from life once in a while so I did find it stressful dealing with the everyday running of the business and becoming consistent, this is something that we will learn to manage ourselves which is why one of the most important part of business is remaining healthy so stay in tune with your body, listen to what it says, if you feel like resting an extra hour and you're not going to miss an appointment then relax and chill, your health is one of the most important marketing tool that you will ever have, I personally eat a lot of fruits and vegetables plus a lot of smoothie making. A great thing to remember is the things that are out of your control should never control you; we can find ways to let these things go as they can damage the life we are aiming to create.

Shop windows has been a good form of getting new clients, whatever your business idea you should be able to market it there, this is one of my best ways of marketing so I keep doing it and it only cost £1 a week to place an advert.

I developed a table of all the advertisement streams that I used then indicated which client came from which stream therefore I know which is the best stream to invest more time with, with the shop windows I write all the shops names that I have advertised in , some shops do not bring back results, to find out how your customer found you, just ask them when they call or email, once or twice I forgot to ask but I got hoover it eventually, now I ask every time and all you have to say is where did you see or hear about us?

I developed a few websites a couple of years ago with Yola (homezonecleaning.yolasite.com) feel free to check it out! once I realised my definite purpose of opening a cleaning business I decided to redo my website as a cleaning website, I have received inquires and new clients from this method, the page I choose has a page where potential customers fill in their personal information then once they submit, their information then arrives in my email inbox, such a great engine that works like a gem for absolutely free. Some customers ask that you contact them back via email so I do exactly that, the customers that do not specify then I just text them to start finding out more about their cleaning needs. When I used to get email inquiries I used to email the individuals back although it seems that emails aren't necessarily at the top of a persons' priority list, often when emails are sent it could go into the persons' junk folder. At first when I started I felt that I would be imposing on a customer if I just sent them a text message or rang them maybe I have low self esteem/confidence however this is something that I can and am working on, it's all a part of life. I took a leap of faith eventually and started texting back the clients which have worked out just fine and all the customers that inquire have been absolutely lovely.

Picture of my current website, this is the main page

Picture of part of the contact us page

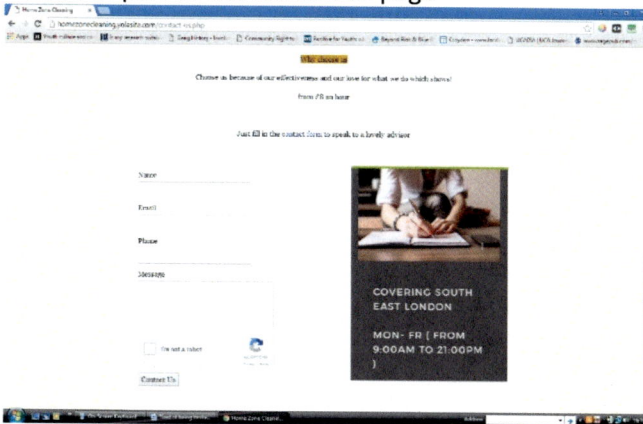

For me obtaining a website was important as it can work on my behalf 24 hours a day, I always include my website address on all my marketing items such as my business cards, flyers, online adverts as this helps to drive traffic (extra business) to the website. I have recently got something called Google business, I have not used it much although I do think it will be a great tool , once I add more facilities (information) then further growth will occur, let's see if my prediction is right (so I received a call after I wrote this section from a lady in Beckenham, I asked her how she heard about us as I thought she was a recommendation, I was very surprised to hear that she found us on the top of Google's search engine- I'm assuming this is a miracle and was helped by Google business.

This is us being listed on Google as a business, Thank you Google

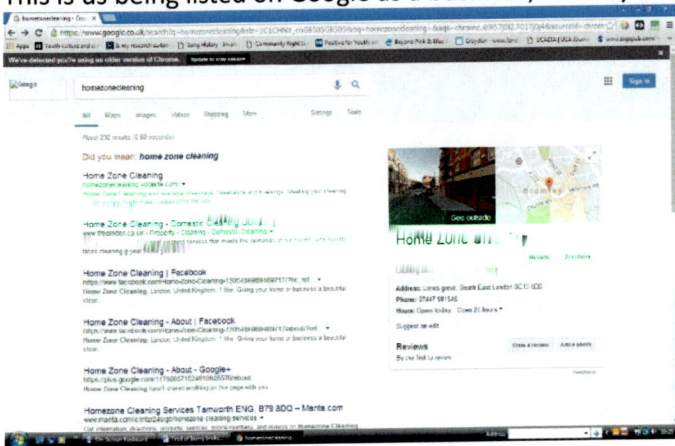

Along with our business cards our websites also need to change as we grow in business we begin to learn more so we make changes to our ways of communicating to our customers for instance I have started to add offices as well as homes to my cleaning cards so my market (people I offer a service to can grow) now I can start putting cards in estate agents as well as cafes, massage places, hairdressers, dry cleaners and other places. I received a call based on a card that I had put in a Chinese massage shop in Penge while with my friend Koleena who runs a social enterprise "Freeway Union Link Up" so I know it works, I've seen a few new spots that I can place some cards, like I placed a card at the Dex building in Ladywell, it used to be a leisure centre. I have been doing slightly less recently now it's winter, it's very cold, Christmas is under 10 days away, the best thing is I know I will get it done, I always do, this point was written after the previous point was recorded and now I am consciously doing more for myself and the business and making sacrifices where possible to be able to accomplish my goals, if that means staying up 10 minutes later then so be it, the only moment we have is the now so we need to cultivate it, sometimes we need to become more productive in order to successfully grow, if this months goals are larger than last months then we have to do things differently to get different results, I choose to do it the smart way, like Deepak Chopra says it's all about the law of least effort, I listen to his affluence audio book on you tube and it definitely creates great results in transforming the way I view business life and wealth.

I am the marketing manager, the administrator, the telephone operator for the business so doing things in its simplest forms by using systems that works helps to make sure my bills get paid, I have enough pocket money that I use to invest back in the business as you have heard I have not spent a lot on developing the business which doesn't mean I won't in the future, I am a woman who knows how to use a shoe string budget to obtain great results. So you have heard me mention business cards, luckily I have a printer and a laptop, I have a printer that I am able to order refurbished ink from Amazon which are more cost effective than buying new ink, some printers are not compatible with reusable inks, I always buy photo paper or colored card from the pound shop, I am able to print my window ads and normally fit 3 adverts on one piece of paper which I then cut to seize, I also obtain images from Google to use on these adverts and have Googled cleaning ads to get more ideas to use for my own advertising. I am planning on upgrading my business cards, vista print offers around 500 business cards for £12.99, sometimes they have really good promotions other than that it's still reasonably priced, I have used vista print in the past and know they are good. My home printed cards works perfectly fine and now I am improving my brand image as you do, since I wrote the last statement I have upgraded my business cards which look really professional and I intent to get some flyers printed for my shop window ad again to give my business a professional edge with the intention of obtaining more customers   Since I wrote this section last I have found that using my professional cards has not brought me much success in shop windows so I will return to my home printed adverts and see if that makes a difference.

I have a yell.com advert which is £12.00 a month so its one of my larger business expenses, because of the previous clients I have obtained from this marketing stream , yell.com has already paid for itself luckily, however it is not something I would renew, it ends in may and there is not a regular monthly customer turnover , I know I will find a better stream to invest this £12 into, this is the thing sometimes I have a budget to play with however I won't invest in just in any marketing strategy as if it does not yield the right returns I will be annoyed so I choose wisely when advertising and I have provided employment for over 10 people so far and have kept my stress level way down, I intent to continue this way because the relationship between me and my business is very important and I want me and Home Zone Cleaning to remain friends.

So I have given you the marketing tips I use which should get you a few clients, remember you have to approach marketing with the right attitude in order to see results, always believe you will do it and you will even when sometimes the clients start to dry up and the phone is not ringing, do not give up just keep learning new ideas via Google, Facebook, you tube or other places or people because with this attitude the light bulb moments will occur.

Chapter 5: Mindset and goal setting

How you Set your Mind, How have you set yours? Do you believe you can achieve anything you desire or do you often doubt yourself?

I believe I can and will achieve my goals and at times I truly doubt myself, the key for me is when I doubt myself I ask myself why am I feeling this way, normally this happens because a strategy isn't giving me the outcome I had hope for, then I start to doubt the overall success of the business, then often I realize that I'm doing something new so of course I may not get everything right the first time and not only that, sometimes we have to be patience in order to see the results so if I begin doubting myself and not waiting to see the result it's likely that I may even quit. Mindsets are something that should and can be developed. I am my business, Vincent Norman Peale speaks of the importance of thinking positively and how that influences our realities.

Ok so thinking positively is key so is being courageous and strong which was a message from my brother Mikey and knowing that this strength and courageous isn't done by us, I try to remember that I did not make myself , fair enough my mum and dad helped, however none of us on our own could make the life forms we have today so within my business I acknowledge that yes I make decisions that often result in receiving customers, however I acknowledge that I am not the only one to thank, I thank the creator who made this and other planets.

For me by respecting God I find that I can obtain more. When I action my business steps I do it in faith knowing that I will see positive results I pray for the strength and courageous to be able to picture myself reaching my goals, I need will power and determination to continue, if you see this book online or in reality just know that you too will become resourceful enough to realize and achieve your goals and aspiration. A great way to stay grounded is to remember why you are doing what you are choosing to, for no fault of your own sometimes, things will go wrong as Mr and Mrs Islam says there is always balance good doesn't exist without the bad. The more interesting point for me is how our mind is set when things are going badly, if your mind is set on a positive dial then stress and joy becomes manageable.

I once learnt

Positive =Increases life force energy My percentage 60%	Negative =Decreases life force energy My percentage 40%

A good tool would be to write what percentage you are.

It is a good measuring tool so we can see exactly where we are and how we may possibly become better- do not feel bad if your percentage isn't where you want it to be as that will only help to lower your life force energy.

My percentages weren't always like that, when I am too negative I do not like how it feels, I at times have become a victim and was unable to see how to change my situation: In business I choose to be more confident and conquer however there is still a lot of things I should be doing, I'm sure that I will and am finding great solutions to become more focused and driven.

EXAMPLE:

My Facebook marketing is going well, most of my strategies has good growth potential, (you should have noticed the confidence in that statement), that confidence stems from me seeing results, all the negative mindset I have doesn't just go away instantly, I decided to have a more positive outlook on life, I know I carry a lot of past hurts whether from other people telling me that I wouldn't reach very far in life or me telling myself negative things, these past hurts can result in unnecessary outbursts therefore every new victory helps to heal past damages. My new failures are reframed as learning tools so I can not only have a temporary solution but rather a long term solution to living a positive, inspiring and motivated life.

Prior to this I didn't have the confidence to do the please like and share this video, often you will hear this being said at the end of a kool video or the bottom of a cool Facebook post. The change in confidence was the fact that I started a Facebook group "Home Zone Cleaning" which I haven't promoted, Facebook notified me that it had its first view, so then I wrote my very first post from my group to mark the occasion, I asked my friends to like and share my post which made me feel empowered, if you are already doing these things and feel that I am a whimp then good on you(lol).

Your mind is constantly with you that is why it is important to train it and never let anyone else do it for you. To try and develop this information effectively I will tell you my story, born and raised in a playground where I spent most of my days in sunny Jamaica, paradise, I moved to the UK did most of my schooling and made plenty of great friends, I choose not to go to university as that made no sense, I worked in a good establishment but knew I couldn't do it forever, seemed like a death sentence, so glad that many people don't feel that way about work otherwise this world would be so different, I'm

unsure of whether it would be better or worst. I eventually went to university for three year and studied Social Enterprise which was life changing as I stated previously I started other enterprises whether it was selling my left over dinners at work or doing people's hair however I became lost in the impurities and injustices of this world, I felt as if I lost my purpose, amongst all these wars and people starving, what or how could I be a part of this, even though as a person who got many people to donate to charity that doesn't take away the distaste of our civilization , luckily I was given a book by Rick Warren which brought me back to life "a purpose driven life" sparked within me a great bright light where I was able to write down my goals and plan a future, I re created my purpose now I still have days where I feel deflated and unmotivated so I listen to motivational speakers or talk with friends or acquaintance where I gain more wisdom knowledge and understanding.

There are so many individuals that I love to listen to like Deepak Chopra (affluence), Les brown is amazing and after listening to him I

decided that he is my adopted father, Bob proctor is amazing and there are vast amounts of useful videos on you tube.

Back to our mindsets if you are lacking in marketing then Google marketing strategies or you tube how to market your business online, tuns and tuns of information will be available, once the wealth of your mind grows so will your physical wealth as your thoughts are creating your reality which comes from the bible or the secrets, it's all the same thing what you focus on will grow.

The law of attraction is me, I attract what I put out there so If I don't put my adverts out or speak to people about my business then it's likely I may get the odd person that comes up to me and says that I need a cleaner (lol) seriously that can happen, so lets set our Goals

and achieve them by breaking them down into bite seize goals with detailed action plans even when your head and mind says you will fail see beyond that.

Have faith and be of great courage

So much resources is out there so choose HOPE today choose LIFE and CREATE YOU, a better you than the one from yesterday.

God bless, live long and strong and be a prosperous enterprise which trades ethnically

WHY: BECAUSE YOU AS AN INDIVIDUAL IS A BUSINESS AND HOW WE MANAGE THIS WILL DETERMINE HOW YOU SET YOUR MIND AND YOUR LIFE FORCE

- I WOULD LIKE TO THANK MY GRANDMOTHERS MY MOTHER MY FATHER MY BROTHERS AND SISTERS AUNTIES UNCLES COUSINS NEPHEWS AND NIECES, TO ALL OF FAMILY- I LOVE YOU, THANK YOU FOR ALL YOUR PRAYERS AND GUIDEANCE.

- THANKS TO ALL MY OTHER MOTHERS WHO SAW ME AS THEIR CHILD...IM LIKEABLE...LOL

- BIG UP JEFF, YOU'RE THE MAN

- THANKS TO MR AND MRS WILSONS FOR INSPIRING ME

- BIG UP D

- THANK YOU TO ALL THOSE WHO ALLOW ME TO CLEAN FOR THEM IT IS SUCH A JOY HAVING SUCH POSITIVE AND ANGELIC CUSTOMERS

- THANK YOU TO THE VERY PEOPLE THAT HAVE CREATED AN EXTENSION TO HOME ZONE CLEANING.

- THANKS TO NATURES CROWN FOR THE INSPIRATIONAL PRODUCTS AND LOVE WWW.NATURESCROWN.CO.UK GREAT SKIN AND HAIR PRODUCTS

- KAIZY STEWART CHECK HER OUT ON YOUTUBE SHE IS WONDERFUL
- CHECK OUT DREAM CLEAN ON GOOGLE, GREAT CLEANING COMPANY
- THANK YOU TO LIFE AND MOTHER EARTH
- BIG UP STAMMA KID FOR THE GREAT MUSIC- CHECK OUT YOU TUBE !
- RONY BRASI BONES IS A GREAT ARTIST, CHECK ME OUT ON FACEBOOK! BANGING TUNES
- GERHARD X AMUNYOKO YOU ARE AMAZING
- MZ GHETTE I LOVE YOUR STYLE OF MUSIC
- FRESHTY FRESH YOUR CLOTHES LINE IS AMAZING
- MAJOR YOU ARE A SUPERSTAR
- BIG UP JERMAIN SIMMS HIS WONDERFUL SON AND ALL THE   FAMILY
- SHOGUN FILES YOU ARE A MAN OF TRUE INTELLECT
- BIG UP RAS JAHSON FOR YOUR TEACHINGS
- BLESS UP ISH FOR YOUR KINDNESS
- FREEWAY UNION LINK UP- THANK YOU FOR CREATING SOCIAL PLATFORMS THAT BRING PEOPLE TOGETHER
- REN YOU ARE A WISE YOUNG MAN AND YOU CONTINUE TO MAKE EVERYONE PROUD

I WANT TO SAY A VERY BIG THANK YOU TO TITO APPAH FOR GIVING ME THE BOOK THE PURPOSE DRIVEN LIFE BY RICK WARREN, IT WAS A KIND AND IMPRESSIVE GESTURE, IT GAVE ME LIFE AND FREEDOM, I THANK GOD OUR CREATOR FOR PROVIDING SUCH A MAN AS THIS TO HELP PROVIDE HOPE FOR OUR WORLD, HIS STORY ALONE SHOWS HIS STRENGTH AND COURAGE "9 LIVES THE TITO APPAH STORY" IS AN INSPIRATIONAL FILM TO WATCH. HIS LOVE FOR BUSINESS IS CONTAGIOUS AND CAN BE SEEN VIA THE MONA LISA GLOBAL BESPOKE PROTRAITS COMPANY WHICH HE OWNS. A STRONG AND WISE MAN WHO HAS AND WILL CONTINUE TO HELP MANY, NO WONDER HE LOVES HIS FAMILY SO MUCH, SURE THEY HAVE PLAYED AN IMPORTANT ROLE IN HIS LIFE ENSURING THAT HE IS SUCESSFUL

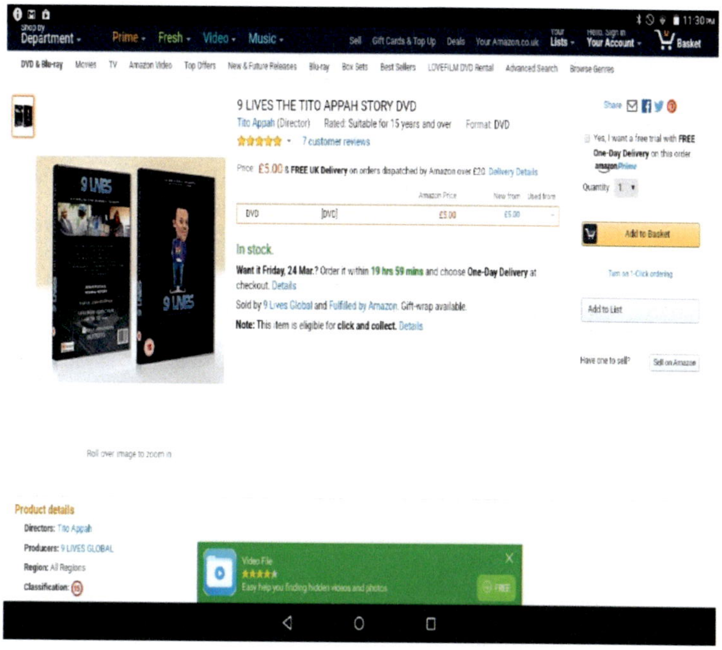

Check out 9 LIVES THE TITO APPAH STORY, AVAILABLE ON AMAZON

Peace love and harmony stay blessed xx
Love always Shernese xx

Made in the USA
Columbia, SC
15 July 2017